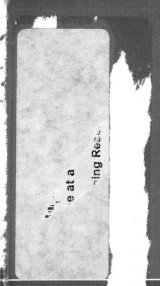

backstage pass

ckstage at a
MUSIC VIDEO

Holly Cefrey

HIGH
interest
books

Children's Press®
A Division of Scholastic Inc.
New York / Toronto / London / Auckland / Sydney
Mexico City / New Delhi / Hong Kong
Danbury, Connecticut

Book Design: Daniel Hosek and Christopher Logan
Contributing Editor: Jennifer Silate

Photo Credits: Cover © S.I.N./Corbis; p. 4 © Douglas Kirkland/Corbis;
p. 7 © Rune Hellestad/Corbis; pp. 8, 15, 18 © Neal Preston/Corbis;
p. 11 © Loomis Dean/TimePix; p. 12 © Bettmann/Corbis; p. 17 © Lynn
Goldsmith/Corbis; p. 21 © Corbis; p. 22 © Reuters NewMedia Inc./Corbis;
pp. 25, 28, 30, 36 Cindy Reiman; p. 26 © Roger Ressmeyer/Corbis;
p. 32 © Anthony Bannister: Gallo Images/Corbis; p. 35 © Steve Raymer/
Corbis; p. 39 Rosen Publishing; p. 41 Maura B. McConnell

Library of Congress Cataloging-in-Publication Data

Cefrey, Holly. WR - 15 46
   Backstage at a music video / Holly Cefrey.
   p. cm.—(Backstage pass)
   Includes bibliographical references and index.
   ISBN 0-516-24324-1 (lib. bdg.)—ISBN 0-516-24386-1 (pbk.)
   1. Music videos—Production and direction—Juvenile literature. 2.
Music videos—History and criticism—Juvenile literature. I. Title. II.
Series.

PNPN1992.8.M87 C44 2003
791.45'6—dc21

                                                      2002007283

CONTENTS

Music videos help performers connect with their audiences in a visually powerful way. Many performers "flip" at the chance of making a video.

Introduction

The band Out Loud is making a new music video for their song "Crush," and you have been hired to direct it! You have worked for weeks preparing to film the video. The costumes are made, the set is built, the dancers are ready, and it's finally time to film.

Everyone is on the set. The dancers are in their places. They have been rehearsing their moves with the choreographer for weeks. The lighting is just right and the cameras are rolling. You signal for the recording of the music to start. The music booms out of huge speakers. The dancers groove and shake to the beat as they sing along to the music. You tell one camera operator to zoom in and focus on the dancers. Another camera operator is farther back from the dancers. She listens to your directions while getting a shot of the whole set. When the dancers have finished their routine, you yell, "Cut!" The first scene of the music video has been filmed. Now, it's time to switch sets and film the band performing "Crush."

By the end of the day, you will be finished filming the entire video. All of your hard work and planning is finally paying off! It won't be long before viewers will be seeing your video on television and singing along to Out Loud's first big hit.

Do you like watching music videos? Have you ever wondered how a music video is made? Read on to find out what goes on behind the scenes of a music video.

Some of the most exciting music videos ever made include a band's concert footage. Watching one of these videos is like being at a live, rocking performance!

Bands that aren't caged in by a low budget are free to use elaborate sets in their videos.

CHAPTER ONE

Video History

Music videos have become an important part of the music industry. Exciting sets, great special effects, and a funky style can make an artist—and his or her song—unforgettable. A great video can take an artist to the top of the music charts. Hundreds of performers have gone from unknowns to superstars with the help of one great music video.

ILLUSTRATED SONGS

The inspiration for today's music videos began in the late 1890s. George Thomas was the first to put photographic images and music together. He photographed people acting out a performance of a song called "The Little Lost Child." The images were printed on slides. Each slide was handpainted to give it color. Musicians in the theater performed the song as the slides were projected onto a screen. This combination of pictures and music was called an illustrated song. At one time, about ten thousand theaters across the United States were showing illustrated songs.

LONG LIVE ROCK AND ROLL!

The first regular TV broadcast began in 1939. At that time, there were only a few hundred TV sets in the United States. Over time, more and more people started owning TV sets. By 1950, there were about six million televisions in homes across the United States. In the early days, most of the music that was aired on television was for adults.

By the mid-1950s, a huge craze was sweeping the nation: rock and roll. Shows such as *American Bandstand* started showing a variety of musical acts that teenagers enjoyed. By 1958, millions of people were watching *American Bandstand* every week. The television was becoming an important source for music.

Television helped to introduce the Beatles' music to people in the United States. On February 9, 1964, the Beatles appeared on *The Ed Sullivan Show*. Their performance is thought to be one of the most important moments for rock and roll on television. More than seventy-three million people watched the Beatles that night. American teenagers went

Dick Clark, the host of the show *American Bandstand*, brought rock and roll into millions of homes every week for 30 years. Young people could groove to the rhythms of their favorite performers on television.

crazy for the band from England. As rock and roll became more popular, television was used to introduce more bands to teenagers. Music on television was no longer just for adults.

Even movies began to shape the future of music videos. The 1964 Beatles' film *A Hard Day's Night*

From left to right: Paul McCartney, John Lennon, Ed Sullivan, George Harrison, and Ringo Starr. After the Beatles conquered America on *The Ed Sullivan Show*, other British bands followed in their footsteps, starting the British Invasion.

was the inspiration for many music videos. The film's use of slow motion, quick edits, and other new film techniques helped to blend the movie's images with the music that the Beatles were playing.

During the 1960s and 1970s, TV shows, such as *The Monkees* and *The Partridge Family*, featured musicians as the stars. Bands also started making videos for their songs. Michael Nesmith, a member of the Monkees, created a half-hour TV show called *Popclips*. *Popclips* showed videos of popular-music artists. In 1980, he sold the show to a company called Warner Amex. The company used the *Popclips* idea to create the Music Television Network (MTV).

I Want My Music Television Network

On August 1, 1981, at 12:01 A.M., MTV became the first music-based TV channel. MTV aired back-to-back music videos. The first video to air was the Buggles' "Video Killed the Radio Star." Within a few months, over two million people were watching MTV. In two years, more than ten million homes received MTV.

Trade Secret

After the success of MTV, the popular 1980s show *Miami Vice* was originally going to be called *MTV Cops*. The creators wanted to combine music with the show. Even though the MTV name wasn't used, some episodes were written around one song, such as Glenn Frey's "Smuggler's Blues."

Other stations started showing music videos, too. In 1983, the Country Music Television Network (CMT) began showing music videos for country-music fans. Video Hits 1 (VH1) was started by the owners of MTV on January 1, 1985. VH1 was created for adult music lovers. In 1995, the Great American Country network (GAC) started showing music videos, too. Today, there are different music video channels and programs around the world, such as MuchMusic from Canada and Channel V from Australia.

The hosts of video-TV shows are called video jockeys, or VJs. The first MTV VJs were (from left to right) Alan Hunter, Martha Quinn, Mark Goodman, Nina Blackwood, and J.J. Jackson.

THRILLING VIDEOS

In 1983, Michael Jackson's "Thriller" video pushed music videos to a new level. "Thriller" cost about $800,000 to make. It was more like a short movie. The video featured elaborate costumes, makeup, and special effects. At first, MTV was not going to air the video. They thought that the 14-minute video was too long. However, Jackson's record company convinced MTV to show the video. "Thriller" soon became the most popular video on MTV. The *Thriller* album sold more than

Trade Secret

Michael Jackson holds the record for the most expensive video ever made. It cost about $7,000,000 to make his video for the song "Scream." He spent more than $10,000 a day just on makeup!

800,000 copies in one week. Record companies saw how much a popular video could boost album sales. They began including money to make music videos in their budgets. Sometimes, record companies spend hundreds of thousands of dollars making one music video.

Music videos have become more interesting and complex over time. Special effects are common in music videos today. As film and sound technology becomes more advanced, so do music videos. Some of the same special effects techniques that are used in movies are also used to make music videos. Award-winning directors, such as Spike Jonze, have worked to make music videos more fantastic.

Michael Jackson's groundbreaking videos helped to make him one of the most popular performers of all time.

Bruce Springsteen (right) discusses his video for "Streets of Philadelphia" with director Jonathan Demme (left). Springsteen and Demme decided to give the video a raw quality to reflect the mood of the song.

CHAPTER TWO

Behind the Camera

A great amount of planning, preparation, and work goes into making a music video. Before shooting the video, many things must be done, such as creating the budget, scheduling the shoot, and hiring crewmembers. One of the first decisions to be made is how much money to spend.

THE POWER OF THE BUDGET

In many cases, the video budget is decided when an artist or a band first signs a recording contract with a record company. Many companies will pay to make a video but deduct the cost of making the video from the artist's or band's earnings.

Record companies may spend $300,000 to $600,000 on a video for a major artist or band. The number of locations and the size of the crew are based on how much money will be spent on a video. A big-budget music video can involve dozens of crewmembers and sophisticated special effects. A low-budget music video can be made by only two or three people. If a low-budget video is shot right, however, it can be just as exciting as a big-budget video. A simple video may cost about $6,000. It can even be filmed in one day using one location, one camera, and basic lighting equipment. Then it would take about three days of editing to be completed.

MAKING THE VIDEO

There are two basic types of music videos: performance video and concept video. The performance video shows the artists performing the song. The concept video uses images and story lines that may or may not be related to the song. Many videos, however, combine elements of both the performance video and the concept video.

The idea for a video can come from the artist, the record company, or the video's director. Many directors develop ideas for a video by just listening to the song. Some directors will then write a treatment. A treatment is a written plan for the video. The treatment is used to give the record company and the artist an idea of how the director would like the video to look. Sometimes, several directors will submit treatments to a record company for one song. The record company chooses the treatment that it likes best. Some videos, such as Moby's "Southside," were done without treatments. Director Joseph Kahn explained his idea for the

David Bowie has used some unusual props and costumes in his concept videos.

"Southside" video into Moby's voice mail. Sometimes, directors are given jobs if they have already made videos that the record company or the artist likes.

Moby won the 2001 MTV Video Music Award for Best Male Video for his song "Southside."

The Crew

Having the right crew can make or break a music video. The crew is responsible for building and lighting the set, doing the artist's makeup, filming the video, and much more. Usually, the treatment that the record company and artist agree on determines what will be done in the music video. However, the crew's decisions, skills, and input on the project are very important and add to the success of the video.

Preproduction

After the treatment is approved, the planning begins. First, a storyboard is made. The storyboard is a set of drawings of each scene in the video. Sometimes, a director will work with a storyboard artist whose job it is to draw storyboards. The storyboard shows what the director wants the video to look like. The director follows it as a guide when he films the video. Once the look and feel of the video is decided, the location for filming the video must be determined. A location manager finds a suitable place for shooting the video. When the director approves the location, the location manager must get permission from residents, businesses, and police in the area to film there. Sometimes, special permits to shoot a video are needed. The location manager is responsible for getting these permits by the time shooting begins.

The producer of the video has many jobs. He or she helps to schedule the shoot, makes sure expenses don't go over the budget, and oversees the hiring of the crew and performers. A casting agent is often used to hire performers that may be needed in the video. The director can approve or reject any casting decisions.

Before the day of the shoot, the director decides on the different camera angles that will be used in the video. The director may also work closely with a director of photography (DP). The DP chooses the cameras and film to be used in the video. The DP also makes sure that the lighting and the camera movement is right. Sometimes, the DP operates a camera, too. However, in larger video productions, a camera operator is hired to do that.

Production Time

On the day of the shoot, many people work to make sure that everything goes as planned. Often, there is an assistant director who has to keep the cast and crew on schedule. Lighting technicians

Often police will help with traffic during video shoots—if you have a permit.

set up the lights used in the video. Sound technicians are in charge of the playback. The playback
is the song the artist sings along to while the video
is being filmed.

▲ Skilled video editors can make sure a music video
doesn't miss a beat.

In videos that use special effects, such as fog, a visual effects coordinator may be used. The visual effects coordinator is responsible for making sure that all special effects happen as the director instructs. Many other people may work on a big-budget music video set, including a key craft, who is responsible for making sure there is enough food for the cast and crew to eat.

Postproduction

After the video is filmed, it must be edited. This time is called postproduction. The editor works with the director to find the best shots to use. The editor sorts through hours of film to put each scene together as the director wants. If computer effects are needed, computer graphics artists work their magic during postproduction to create the right effects. At every stage, the director and the producer are busy making sure that everything goes as planned. Once the video is finished, it is sent to the record company for approval. Then, it is ready to be aired on music television stations around the world.

After listening to a band's song, a director may be inspired with a great idea for a music video.

CHAPTER THREE

Camera's Rolling, Cue Playback, and...Action!

Directing a music video takes a lot of planning and hard work. Director Layla Sun of Los Angeles, California, describes her experience:

"I have been directing music videos for several years. I heard that ELO Records was looking for someone to direct a music video for a new band called The Refugees. Their song is called "Crooked." I got a copy of the song and listened to it over and over. It's a fun song. There are some really great beats in it, and I liked the singer's voice.

"I spoke with the record company and the lead singer of the band to get an idea of what they had in mind for the video. I also found out what the company's budget is for the video. The record company and the band wanted to have footage of the band performing their song. The Refugees are a new band, so there isn't a very large budget. I decided to use footage of choreographed dancers

A good storyboard will ensure that the director and crew are in tune with each other.

and footage of the band performing in the video. I thought that if we edited the footage of the dancers and the band together in a creative way, the video would look great—and it wouldn't cost too much. Once I had my idea, I wrote the treatment. I wrote down all of my ideas for the video and sent them to the record company.

"My treatment was chosen for the project. As soon as I found out, I started planning the shoot. I sketched a storyboard to get a clear idea of the different shots that I wanted to have in the video. The storyboard really gave me a sense of what the finished video would look like. It was pretty exciting.

"I spoke with my friend, Marcy, who is a choreographer. I was planning to keep the dancing very simple, but energetic. She said that she was working with a great dance company and some of the members were willing to put in some time to work on the video. Next, I had to find a location. We didn't have enough money to hire a location manager, so I looked for some spots myself. Working in the city is expensive and requires a lot of permits. Instead, I called around and found a studio to rent. I found one that was big enough and within our budget. I reserved it for the day of the shoot.

"My friend Lamont has worked as a DP before, and he said that he was free to work on my project. We met to discuss the camera angles that I wanted to have in the video. He recommended some cameras and film that we could use to get the look I wanted. The producer and I hired the rest of the crew: a lighting technician, a sound technician, a camera operator, and an editor. I also arranged for a caterer to provide breakfast and lunch.

The right lighting can really brighten up a music video.

"The day of the shoot has arrived. I work with the DP and the camera operator to get the cameras set up. The lighting technician and the sound technician set up their equipment. At 9:00 A.M., the dancers arrive. They rehearse their moves with the choreographer while the rest of the crew finishes getting things ready. It's 9:30 A.M. and the band still isn't here. Luckily, we are shooting the dance scenes first. However, the band is supposed to be in a few of the dance scenes. They are scheduled to be filmed in an hour! We only have the studio for 10 hours and there is a lot of work to do. I tell the camera operator to start rolling. The sound technician starts the playback and the dancers begin their performance. We do three takes. The camera operators and the DP are pleased with the takes—so am I.

"At 11:00 A.M., the band has finally shown up. They had a show last night and slept late. The band members stretch to wake up and are soon ready to do their scenes. Despite the band's lateness, we are only 30 minutes behind schedule. The camera operators are in position and I tell them to start filming.

The playback starts. The band sings along and performs the dance moves they learned for the video. On the first take, the lead singer gets tripped up and stumbles while dancing. We have to shoot this scene five times to get it right. Next, we shoot the band performing their song with instruments. I get some close-up shots on each of the band members. The lead singer is a good performer. I get a couple of great shots of him singing.

"We finish shooting at 7:00 P.M. I'm tired, but I think we got all of the shots we need for the video. I take the film to a developing center. It will be ready tomorrow. The editor and I will start editing the video as soon as we get it back.

"I meet the editor at the postproduction facility. The video looks good. The color is too bright, but the editor is sure he can fix it. I tell him how I want the shots to be ordered, and we work to get them matched up with the music. It takes us three days to edit the video. Then, I send it off to the record company for approval. I'm really happy with how it turned out. It looks great, and we even managed to stay under the budget!"

WR-1545

Even though they aren't in the spotlight, the crew that works behind the scenes on a music video is just as important as the video's star.

In big cities such as New York and Los Angeles, there are many film schools where students can learn the latest in film technology.

CHAPTER FOUR

Your Life in Video

If you have an interest in directing, lighting, sound, or fashion, making music videos may be for you! There are many ways to get started in the music video industry. Many schools offer classes in film, writing, editing, fashion, graphic design, and other subjects that would be helpful in creating music videos. Some schools, such as the New York Film Academy, even offer workshops for high school students. If you are interested in editing, sound, or graphic design, it's important to know the computer programs that are used by professionals. Even if you get a degree in graphic design, you may still need to take computer courses from time to time to keep up with new programs and technology.

Many people started their music video careers by helping out at video or film production companies after school or during the summer. Some opportunities to work with film may even be available in your community. Offer to help local

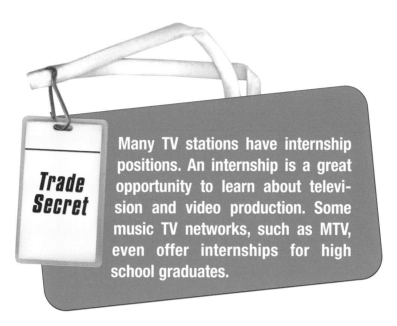

Trade Secret

Many TV stations have internship positions. An internship is a great opportunity to learn about television and video production. Some music TV networks, such as MTV, even offer internships for high school graduates.

production companies in any way that you can. Even if you are just running errands, you will be able to get a feel for the industry and see the kinds of jobs there are in video production. You may also meet people who will know of an opportunity for a better job in the business. If you keep your eyes open and are willing to learn, you could find the job of your dreams.

YOUR FUTURE IS NOW

You can start planning for your career in music videos now. It's never too early to start getting experience. Help out with school plays. High school drama clubs are almost always in need of help. It might not involve video, but working with the lighting, sound, makeup, or costumes in a school play can be a valuable experience.

If you are interested in video production, check to see if your local TV stations offer tours.

Knowing how a camera works is one of the first steps to making a fantastic video.

They may not make music videos there, but they use the same type of equipment that is used for making music videos. You could get a look at the studio and become familiar with the equipment. Learn as much as you can and don't be afraid to ask questions. You can also find information about film techniques and video production in books and magazines, and on videos and the Internet.

DO IT YOURSELF

Want to direct? If you have access to a camera, practice making videos at home. Find a song that you would like to make a video for. Develop a story-board. Plan a shoot. Experiment with lighting and props. Be creative! You can make a great-looking video with very little money. You might be able to get help making videos at your school. Check to see if your school has an audio/visual club. Some schools even have video production equipment. If you use a digital video recorder, there are computer programs that you can use to edit your video. Some video production companies can also help edit your video. Don't limit yourself to just music videos. Many music video directors started out in film and commercials.

The more you know about videos and the more you practice and experiment with video-making, the better chance you'll have at getting a job in music video production. With hard work and determination, you may find yourself backstage at a music video.

Making homemade videos can not only be a great learning experience, but they can be a lot of fun, too.

budget a plan for how money will be spent

camera operator the person in charge of using the camera

choreographer the person who arranges dance steps and movements for a show

concept video a kind of video that has images or a story that may or may not be directly related to the song featured in the video

editor someone in charge of putting a video together by cutting and arranging the film

illustrated song an old form of entertainment that involved showing colored slides along with music

lighting technician the person who sets up and controls the lighting on a set

performance video a kind of video that has an artist or band performing a song

permits written statements giving permission for something

postproduction the time after a film or video has been filmed when editing is done and special effects are added

production a play, an opera, a video, or any other form of entertainment that is presented to others

shoot to film a movie or a video

sound technician the person who sets up and controls the sound on a set

storyboard a set of drawings that shows what the scenes in a filmed production will look like

techniques methods or ways of doing something that requires skill

treatment a written plan for a video

Collier, Maxie D. *The iFilm Digital Video Filmmaker's Handbook*. Los Angeles, CA: Lone Eagle Publishing Company, 2001.

Frantz, John Parris. *Video Cinema: Techniques and Projects for Beginning Filmmakers*. Chicago, IL: Chicago Review Press, 1994.

Hampe, Barry. *Making Documentary Films and Reality Videos*. New York: Henry Holt & Company, Incorporated, 1997.

Sotnak, Lewann. *Director: Film, TV, Radio, and Stage*. Mankato, MN: Capstone Press, 2000.

Organizations

**Association for Independent
Video & Filmmakers
(Foundation for Independent Video and Film)**
304 Hudson Street, 6th floor
New York, NY 10013
(212) 807-1400
Fax: (212) 463-8519
E-mail: info@aivf.org
www.aivf.org

Music Video Production Association
940 N. Orange Drive #104
Hollywood, CA 90038
(323) 469-9494
Fax: (323) 469-9445
E-mail: Musicvideo@aol.com
www.mvpa.com

Web Sites

CMT

www.cmt.com

Read about your favorite country music band and see their video on this Web site.

MTV

www.mtv.com

MTV's Web site has a lot of information about bands and their music videos.

Music Video Insider

www.musicvideoinsider.com

This Web site has a lot of inside information about making music videos.

Music Video Wire

www.mvwire.com

Read interviews with music video directors and learn all about making music videos on this Web site.

INDEX

About the Author

Holly Cefrey is a freelance writer and researcher. She is a member of the Authors Guild and the Society of Children's Book Writers and Illustrators.